Twenty to Make
Wedding Favours

Michelle Powell

Search Press

First published in Great Britain 2008

Search Press Limited
Wellwood, North Farm Road,
Tunbridge Wells, Kent TN2 3DR

Text copyright © Michelle Powell 2008

Photographs by Debbie Patterson at
Search Press Studios

Photographs and design copyright
© Search Press Ltd 2008

ISBN: 978-1-84448-348-8

Suppliers

If you have difficulty in obtaining any of the
materials and equipment mentioned in this book,
then please visit the Search Press website for
details of suppliers: www.searchpress.com

Printed in Malaysia

Dedication
This book is for Mr Ross Goodfield and
Mrs Emma Goodfield, to celebrate their
wedding on July 25th 2008

Contents

Introduction

Wedding favours originate from France and Italy, where aristocrats would give small gifts to their wedding guests called *bonbonnières* to spread good luck. These were small metal or porcelain boxes filled with sugar sweets.

As favours evolved, sugared almonds became the popular choice. They were wrapped in pretty layers of net and decorated with ribbon and flowers. Traditionally, just five sugared almonds would be used, representing fertility, health, wealth, happiness and longevity.

Nowadays almost anything goes and wedding favours can be any small gift given to the guests at a wedding as a token of thanks. Items such as small silver picture frames, candles, wine bottle stoppers or trinket boxes all make great favours, although sweets are still the firm favourite.

This book shows you how you can make your own beautiful wedding favours using basic craft supplies such as coloured card, paper and ribbon. All of the designs can be altered to match your specific colour theme or to suit the feel of the day.

The favours in this book have been designed to be quick to make – even for larger weddings. Where possible craft punches have been used as they are by far the quickest way to cut out shapes, and are more cost effective than purchasing ready-cut flowers or shapes. Remember to leave yourself plenty of time to make your favours as the wedding day approaches.

This book is intended to be a source of inspiration, so feel free to mix and match the designs shown, alter the colours and create variations for christening or party favours. The real joy of making your own favours is that you can create a unique personalised gift for your guests as a memento of your special day.

Tying the Knot

Materials:

Striped cream card
Patterned cream card
Gold card
Wide organza ribbon
Sticky gemstone
Metallic gold thread
Sweets or small gift

Tools:

Small flower punch
Tiny hole punch
Tag punch
All-purpose glue
Scissors
Ruler
Scoring tool

Instructions:

1 Cut an 11.5cm (4½in) square of striped card for the box base and an 8cm (3⅛in) square of patterned card for the box lid.

2 Score lines 3.7cm (1½in) from each edge on all four sides of the square in the centre of the box base. Score lines 1.9cm (¾in) from each edge on all four sides of the square in the centre of the box lid.

3 Referring to the diagram on page 46, use the scissors to cut into the box so that the box base and lid can be folded into shape. Glue the corner tabs and assemble the box.

4 Fill the box with your choice of sweets or a small gift, then put the lid on top. Cut 45cm (17¾in) of wide organza ribbon and tie it around the box, tying a large bow at the top.

5 Punch a tag shape from gold card. Punch a small flower shape and add a gemstone (see detail opposite). Tie it to the bow using a small amount of gold thread.

For a matching **invitation card**, tie 38cm (15in) of wide organza ribbon around a card, made using the same striped card as the box, along with a matching tag to create a co-ordinating piece.

Pin Stripe

Ideal for male guests, this grey and silver version of the project is sleek and stylish. This colour scheme also works well with a splash of hot pink or teal blue.

Party Pail

Materials:

Mini bucket
Pink textured card
Blue card
Spotted organza ribbon
Narrow organza ribbon
Small plastic bag
Sticky gemstone
Glitter
Pink and blue chalks
Flying saucer sweets

Tools:

Heart punch
2.5cm (1in) circle punch
All-purpose glue
Foam pads

Outta Space!

The pretty pastel colours of the flying saucer sweets lend themselves to many candy-coloured combinations. If your wedding colour scheme does not fit, simply change the sweeties to something that will match!

Instructions:

1 Cut 17cm (6¾in) of spotted ribbon and wrap it around the bucket. Attach the ends of the ribbon to the centre front of the bucket using all-purpose glue.

2 Punch a 2.5cm (1in) circle from pink card and a small heart shape from blue card. Colour the edges of each with the pink and blue chalk respectively. Add dots of all-purpose glue to the circle and sprinkle glitter over it.

3 Mount the heart on the circle using foam pads, then attach the sticky gemstone to the heart (see detail opposite).

4 Use foam pads to stick the circle motif in place on the bucket covering the ribbon ends.

5 Fill a 10cm x 5cm (4 x 6in) plastic bag with flying saucer sweets and tie the top with the narrow blue ribbon. Place in the bucket.

Mount a second pink circle and blue heart on a punched 5cm (2in) white circle. Hand write the guest's name on the larger white circle to make a **place card**, and use a mini bulldog clip to hold it in place.

Peacock Paradise

Materials:

Heart-shaped plastic case
Black card
Mirror card
Pink feathers
Pink glitter
Silver-wrapped sweets
Pink wire

Tools:

Large and small heart punches
Glue pen
All-purpose glue
Foam pads
Sticky tape

Instructions:

1 Punch six large hearts from black card and three small hearts from mirror card. Cut three lengths of wire: one 6cm (2¼in), one 8cm (3⅛in) and one 10cm (4in) long.

2 Use a glue pen to draw dots on three of the larger hearts and sprinkle with glitter (see detail opposite).

3 Cover the back of a glittered heart and one of the plain hearts with all-purpose glue. Stick them together, sandwiching the end of one wire between them. Repeat with the other hearts and wires.

4 Mount the small silver hearts on the larger hearts using foam pads.

5 Fill the heart-shaped container with wrapped sweets. Push the ends of two feathers and all three piece of wire into the hole at the back. Twist the wires to secure them in place.

You can make a pink **place card**, and decorate it with matching hearts on wires: simply pierce holes in the fold of the card and insert the wires. Stick them to the inside of the card using sticky tape.

Feather Fancy
Tone down the showgirl look with a subtler colour scheme of beige, gold and burgundy. This design also looks stunning in pure white with silver or gold accents.

Oh, Sweetheart!

Materials:

White chocolate
Lollipop sticks
Clear plastic bag
Wide organza ribbon
Narrow organza ribbon
Heart-shaped beads
Glitter

Tools:

Daisy punch
Pinking shears
Double-sided tape
Double-sided punch tape
Chocolate lollipop mould

Instructions:

1 Punch four daisy shapes from double-sided punch tape. Stick them on the bottom 7cm (2¾in) of the plastic bag.

2 Stick a strip of double-sided tape along the bag opening on both front and back and trim off the excess using pinking shears.

3 Remove the backing from the punched flowers and double-sided tape edge, then sprinkle with glitter. Shake off the excess.

4 Following the manufacturer's directions, fill the mould with melted chocolate, add a lollipop stick and leave in the fridge to set.

5 Cut 16cm (6¼in) of narrow ribbon, add a heart-shaped bead to both ends and knot (see detail).

6 Place the lollipop in the bag and tie with 40cm (15¾in) of wide organza ribbon, knotting in the narrow ribbon as you tie the bow.

To accompany the lollipop, pack a single small heart-shaped **chocolate in a box** with a clear plastic lid. Add narrow ribbon with heart-shaped beads on each end.

12

Burnished

Use milk chocolate with brown glitter for a colour theme variation. Also try adding a little food colouring to white chocolate to make shades of pink, red, green or blue. If you are short on time, use shop-bought chocolate lollipops.

True Blue

Materials:
Light blue card
Mirror card
Glitter
Eyelet
Feather trim
Narrow ribbon
Chalks

Tools:
Circle punch
Heart punch
Cricut personal cutter
Tags, Bags, Boxes, and More
   cartridge (Cricut: 29-0022)
Eyelet setter and hammer
Glue pen
All-purpose glue
Foam pads

Instructions:

1 Use the personal cutter with the cartridge to cut a bag-shaped box from blue card. Alternatively, use a ready-bought box blank.

2 Draw dots using a glue pen on the bag front and sprinkle with matching coloured glitter.

3 Cut two 8cm (3⅛in) lengths of feather trim and stick to each side of the bag using all-purpose glue.

4 Punch a 3.8cm (1½in) circle of mirror card and a heart shape from coloured card. Chalk the edge of the heart and add dots of glitter using a glue pen.

5 Set an eyelet in the top of the circle to create a tag. Stick the heart to the tag using a foam pad and tie the tag to the bag using narrow ribbon.

Make a stylish **pouch** for a thin after-dinner chocolate mint. Decorate the simple pouch with a matching tag and a short piece of feather trim. Remember to punch out a half circle on one side of the pouch so that it is easy to remove the mint.

Note

Personal cutters can cut any shape. You buy a cartridge with about one hundred shapes and select the one you want to cut.

Pure White

For a pretty and soft look vary the colours used to silver and pure white. Decorate your tables with crystal gemstones and white candles wrapped in feather trim for a really romantic wedding theme.

Champagne Supernova

Materials:
Mini bottle of champagne
Purple organza fabric
Gold-striped organza fabric
Tassel
Sewing thread

Tools:
Sewing machine
Scissors
Iron

Instructions:

1 Cut one piece of purple organza fabric and one piece of gold-striped organza fabric, both 25cm x 30cm (9⅞in x 11⅞in).

2 Sew the right sides together along the 30cm (11⅞in) edge. Iron the seam flat and open out.

3 Fold the piece in half in the opposite direction so that the top half is coloured and the bottom half is stripy. Stitch the right sides together along the new longest side.

4 Iron the new seam open and roll the striped organza half down over the coloured organza half.

5 Position the side seam at the centre back and sew the seam at the base of the bag. Turn the bag right sides out.

6 Place the bottle in the bag and add a 10cm (4in) long gold tassel to the bottleneck.

To make a matching **coin stack**, cut two 23cm (9in) diameter circles of fabric using pinking shears, one in each fabric. Stack six chocolate coins and wrap using the organza circles. Tie with narrow ribbon.

Cheers!

Vary the colour of the organza to match your wedding colour scheme. Most wedding dress shops will sell you a length of dress fabric to match yours or your bridesmaid's dresses. Mini bottles of wine are a good alternative to the champagne if your budget is tight.

Delicrystal

Instructions:

1 Cut a rectangle of vellum 24 x 18cm (9½ x 7in) and score every 6cm (2½in) to make a grid of twelve 6cm (2½in) squares (see the diagram on page 47). Fold a valley fold on every score line.

2 Ignore the top row of three squares and focus on the nine squares below. At each of the four corner squares on the nine square grid, score a diagonal line from the centre square to the outside edge. Refer to the diagram on page 47.

3 Fold each of the diagonal score lines with a mountain fold. The vellum will now be creating a box shape.

4 Fold the corner triangles to the front and back of the box and allow the top row of squares to fold in over each other. This creates the flap.

5 Trim 1.5cm (½in) off the edge of the flap using scalloped scissors. Push the sides of the box in and pull the flap over the top to create the triangle shape (see detail opposite).

6 Fill the box with sweets. Cut 50cm (19¾in) of wide ribbon and tie around the box. Stitch on a heart-shaped charm decorated with a sticky gemstone.

Make a matching **napkin ring tag** from a rectangle of card decorated with vellum and a heart charm.

True Romance

Create a colour variation by changing the vellum to a glitter-printed design and the ribbon colour to a rich wine shade, or vary it to match your wedding day's colour theme.

Hidden Diamond

Tools:
All-purpose glue
Scissors

Materials:
White organza bag
Green and white
   ribbon flowers
Pearl stems
Fabric leaf
Green sugared
   almonds
Silver dragées

Instructions:

1 Fill the organza bag with five sugared almonds and a sprinkling of silver dragées.

2 Separate the pearl stems and select five or six. Hold them in front of the fabric leaf and use the wire from the ribbon flower (see detail opposite) to wrap tightly around the ends of the pearl stems and leaf wire.

3 Trim off the ends of the pearl stems and leaf wire. Use all-purpose glue to seal the ends together.

4 Use the remaining flower wire to pierce through one layer of the organza bag in the centre, in front of the ribbon ties.

5 Thread the wire back out to the front and twist around the flower to secure. Trim off the end of the wire and pull up the ribbons to close the bag.

Create a matching **place card** by mounting a ribbon flower and three pearl stems on a folded card rectangle. Hand write or computer print the guest's name below.

The Black Pearl

Use cool, contemporary colours to create this chic and opulent version of the favour bag. Fill with silvered sugar almonds to complete the look.

Here Comes the Bride

Materials:

Textured white card
Silver-coloured card
White glitter card
Glitter
White organza ribbon
Sticky gemstones
Sweets

Tools:

Flower punches
Glue pen
All-purpose glue
Scoring tool
Ruler
Scissors

Instructions:

1 Cut a 18 x 12cm (7 x 4¾in) rectangle of textured white card. Score a horizontal line 4cm (1½in) from the bottom edge.

2 Starting at the left hand edge, score four further vertical lines each 4cm (1½in) apart. This should leave a 2cm (¾in) tab at the right-hand end.

3 Cut along each of the vertical score lines from the bottom edge up to the horizontal score line.

4 Fold mountain folds on all of the score lines to form a tall box shape. Trace the template from page 46 and transfer it onto each side of the box, lining the base of the template up with the horizontal score line.

5 Trim the top of each side of the box off to create the bodice shape. Push in the sides of the box to squash the top section flat.

6 Decorate the bodice with lines of glitter, applied using the glue pen, and a gemstone. Insert your sweets then tie a ribbon around the waist and in a bow at the back (see detail opposite).

7 Punch two flowers from metallic and glitter card. Glue them together and add a gemstone to the centre. Stick in place on the front of the box.

For an accompanying **treat box**, fill a small tin with silver dragées and decorate with ribbon and a punched flower.

Pretty in Pink
Use pink card and glitter to create a bridesmaid dress version of the wedding dress box. You could even reduce or enlarge the box size for younger or older bridesmaids. This box would be ideal to pack their special bridesmaid thank-you gift.

Party Spirit

Materials:

Miniature alcohol bottle
Red card
Cream card
Cream glitter card
Red ribbon
Red inkpad

Tools:

Heart punch
Circle punch
Scroll rubber stamp
All-purpose glue
Foam pads

Instructions:

1 Cut a 5 x 6cm (2 x 2½in) rectangle of cream card. Ink the scroll stamp with coloured ink and stamp the image twice, overlapping.

2 Mount the stamped card on a slightly larger rectangle of coloured card.

3 Glue the label to the front of the bottle and bind with spare ribbon until the glue has dried.

4 Cut a 15cm (6in) length of ribbon and glue around the neck of the bottle, crossing at the front in the centre of the label.

5 Punch a circle of glitter card and a heart shape. Mount the heart on the circle and the circle on the bottle using foam pads.

For an extra favour, wrap a rectangle of stamped card around a **mint chocolate** and decorate with a punched heart and circle motif.

Boozy Bottle

Use shades of cream and olive green for a sophisticated and traditional variation. These decorated bottles are ideal for male guests and could be combined with a more girly favour design for the ladies.

Love Grows

Tools:
Circle punches
Flower punch
Foam pads
Paintbrush
Scissors

Materials:
Cream card
Gold mirror card
Glitter vellum
Narrow ribbon
Mini plant pot
Gold metallic paint
Kebab stick
Wild flower seeds
Net

Instructions:

1 Paint a 3cm (1⅛in) tall mini plant pot and a 7cm (2¾in) length of kebab stick with gold metallic paint and leave to dry.

2 Punch one flower shape from cream card and another from glitter vellum. Curl the petals and stick together using foam pads, sandwiching in the end of the kebab stick.

3 Punch a 1.6cm (¾in) circle of gold metallic card and a 1.2cm (½in) circle of cream card. Mount in the centre of the flower using foam pads.

4 Fill a 15cm (6in) circle of net with wild flower seeds and tie up loosely using narrow ribbon.

5 Place the seeds in the flowerpot and push the kebab stick into the centre of the net. Tie the ribbon more firmly around the stick and net.

Make a **sugared almond favour** to go with the pot. Fill a shallow box lid with sugared almonds and wrap with a glittered net. Decorate with a punched flower as before.

Potty About You

Use shades of pink and silver for a more colourful variation. Any colour would work well with this design. Be sure to match your sugared almond colour too for the full effect.

Dragonfly Display

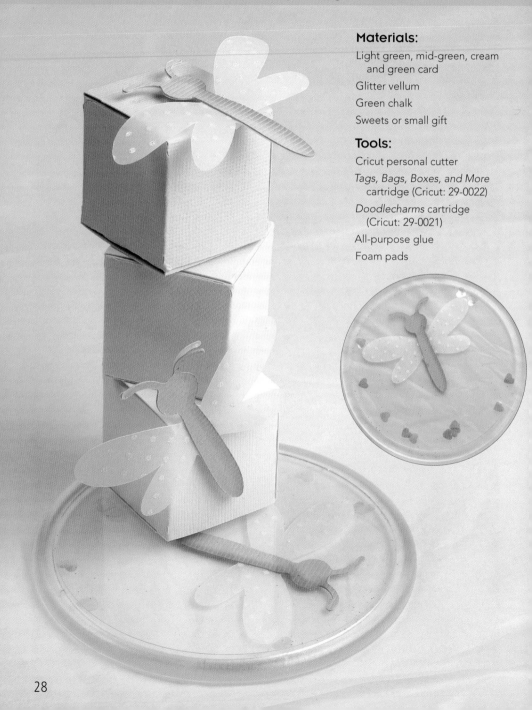

Materials:

Light green, mid-green, cream and green card

Glitter vellum

Green chalk

Sweets or small gift

Tools:

Cricut personal cutter

Tags, Bags, Boxes, and More cartridge (Cricut: 29-0022)

Doodlecharms cartridge (Cricut: 29-0021)

All-purpose glue

Foam pads

Instructions:

1 Cut out three boxes, using the personal cutter with the *Tags, Bags, Boxes, and More* cartridge and light green, cream and mid-green card. Alternatively, you can use ready-made boxes.

2 Assemble each box, gluing the tabs, and fill with your choice of sweet, or a small gift.

3 Use the personal cutter with the *Doodlecharms* cartridge to cut two dragonfly shapes from glitter vellum and two dragonfly body shapes from green card.

4 Chalk the edges of the dragonfly bodies and glue in place on the vellum wings. Stack three boxes and attach the dragonflies using foam pads.

To make an accompanying **coaster**, place one dragonfly image and a sprinkling of confetti hearts inside a plastic drinks coaster (see detail opposite).

Wonderful Winged Centrepiece

For a really impressive look, choose shades of purple and pink and display your favour boxes in a large stack on a silver platter as a table centrepiece. Alternatively, you could fill the boxes with after-dinner chocolates and serve with the coffees.

Eternal Blossom

Materials:

Take-away style box

Light blue, dark blue
   and white card

Spotted ribbon

Blue wire

Sticky gemstones

Sugared almonds

Tools:

Flower punches

Small circle punch

Stamen punch

Wire cutter

Round-nosed pliers

Ball-tipped stylus and craft foam

All-purpose glue

Instructions:

1 Fill the take-away style box with sugared almonds, then wrap the ribbon around it and glue the ribbon on to the base.

2 Punch three large flowers from dark blue card, three smaller flowers from light blue card and three stamens from white card. Burnish each of the pieces using the ball-tipped stylus to give a cupped shape.

3 Assemble the flowers using all-purpose glue and add a sticky gemstone to the centre of each (see detail opposite).

4 Cut 22cm (8½in) of wire and spiral both ends using round-nosed pliers. Wrap the wire around the left-hand side of the box handle.

5 Punch three small circles from the dark blue card. Glue the flowers in place on the wire, and use glue to attach a circle behind each flower, sandwiching in the wire.

Make a pretty **wine glass decoration**. Cut 18cm (7in) of wire, spiral both ends and bend into shape. Glue on two punched flowers made in the same way as before and hang the piece from the side of a wine glass filled with sweets.

Far East

A lemon and lime green colour scheme creates an oriental look for this favour box and wine glass decoration.

Cutting the Cake

Materials:

Ingredients for a cake, or
shop-bought mini cake

Cake board

Cellophane wrap

Wide pink organza ribbon

Narrow pink organza ribbon

Silver metallic card

Small elastic band

Tools:

Heart punch

All-purpose glue

Scissors

Instructions:

1 Make a decorated mini cake about 7cm (2¾in) in diameter. Mount it on a 10cm (4in) diameter cake board.

2 Cut out a square of cellophane wrap 40 x 40cm (15¾ x 15¾in). Place the cake in the middle, pull the wrap up the sides and use a small elastic band to secure the top.

3 Punch two heart shapes from metallic card, then turn the card over and punch two more (to allow the non-symmetrical heart shapes to line up perfectly).

4 Cut 16cm (6¼in) of narrow ribbon and glue two hearts to each end, sandwiching the ribbon between.

5 Cut 80cm (31½in) of wide ribbon and tie it around the neck of the wrapping. As you tie a large bow, catch in the narrow ribbon.

Create just the **hanging hearts** (see steps 3 and 4) and use a mini peg (see detail opposite) to attach them to a napkin or the side of a wine glass for extra decoration.

Bake a Cake

Ice your cakes in a rich cream shade and pack in gold-printed cellophane with a cream bow for a more traditional wedding colour scheme.

33

Cinders' Bag

Materials:

Pink card

Pink glitter card

Silver metallic card

Sticky gemstone

Glitter

Vellum

Tools:

Cricut personal cutter

Tags, Bags, Boxes, and More cartridge (Cricut: 29-0022)

All-purpose glue

Flower punches

Oval punch

Glue pen

Foam pad

Instructions:

1 Use the personal cutter and cartridge to cut a handbag box shape from pink card. Assemble the bag by gluing the tabs.

2 Punch an oval of pink card and fold in half. Add a glue pen line to the front half and sprinkle with glitter.

3 Glue the back half of the oval to the back face of the bag and bend the glittered half down on the front to make the bag's flap.

4 Punch the larger flower shape once from metallic card and once from vellum and the smaller flower from glitter card.

5 Bend up the petals of each flower and assemble using all-purpose glue (see detail opposite). Add a sticky gemstone in the centre and stick in place on the bag.

To make a fun **shoe favour**, fill a net with silver dragées and tie the top with narrow ribbon. Place in a clear plastic shoe shape and decorate with a punched flower made in the same way as the first.

Shoes 'n' Bags
Use super trendy shades of teal blue and silver to make a classy variation on the handbag and shoe favours.

A Real Lime Wire

Materials:

Green card

Glitter card

Glitter

Spotted ribbon

Large brad

Metal tin with clear lid

Sugared almonds

Tools:

Flower punch

Circle punch

Foam pads

All-purpose glue

Instructions:

1 Punch a flower shape from coloured card and bend forward the petals. Punch a circle from glittered card.

2 Cover the top of a large brad with glue and sprinkle with glitter. Leave to dry, and then assemble the flower using the brad.

3 Fill a metal tin with sugared almonds or sugar-coated chocolates and tie 45cm (17¾in) of ribbon around the tin in a bow on the top.

4 Fix the flower on the lid of the tin, next to the ribbon, using two sticky foam pads (see detail opposite).

Make a matching **place card** using a 10 x 7cm (4 x 2¾in) piece of card, folded in half. Add a punched flower and a ribbon trim.

Funky Flower Tin

The acid shades of lime and white create a bold and bright colour combination ideal for young fun weddings, but subdued pastel pinks and purples work well for a more traditional look.

Clear to be True

Tools:
All-purpose glue
Stamp punch
Heart punch
Foam pads

Materials:
Clear plastic box
Sticky gemstones
Mini marshmallows
Narrow ribbon
Glitter card
Pink card
Vellum

Instructions:

1 Fill a 4cm (1½in) clear cube box with mini marshmallows. Cut a 2.5cm (1in) strip of vellum and wrap around the box, gluing it at the base.

2 Cut 17cm (6¾in) of narrow ribbon and glue around the box in the centre of the vellum.

3 Punch a heart shape from glitter card and a stamp shape from pink card. Add a sticky gemstone to the top of the heart.

4 Fix the heart to the stamp shape using a foam pad and fix in place on the front of the box.

To make an accompanying **place card**, cut an 8 x 9cm (3⅛ x 3½in) rectangle of pink card and fold in half. Decorate with a strip of vellum and a punched motif to match the favour box.

Black 'n' white

This simple design will work in any colour scheme and looks stunning in the black, silver and white combination shown here. It could also look striking in gold and black or shades of red.

Pure Gold

Materials:

Organza bag
Coloured vellum
Glitter-dotted net
Cream heart-shaped button
Metallic thread
Gold sugared almonds

Tools:

Flower punch
Needle

Instructions:

1 Fill an organza bag with five sugared almonds.

2 Punch a flower shape from coloured vellum and hand cut a circle shape, 6cm (2¼in) in diameter, from glitter net.

3 Thread a needle with metallic thread and stitch the heart-shaped button to the net and vellum flower shape (see detail opposite).

4 Stitch the flower to the organza bag in the centre of the pull cord casing, catching only the front layer of fabric.

Decorate a glass with sticky gemstones and a matching punched flower. Place a battery-powered **votive candle** inside and wrap with matching vellum to complete the look.

Bold Bloom Bag

Use cool shades of silver and blue to make this variation on the bag and candle votive.

The Secret Treat!

Materials:
White card
Gold metallic card
Brown card
Sticky pearls
Narrow brown ribbon

Tools:
Flower punches
Scalloped scissors
All-purpose glue
Foam pads
Scissors
Scoring tool
Ruler

Instructions:

1 Following the directions for the Tying the Knot project on pages 6–7 (see also page 46), make three boxes with the following dimensions:

Bottom tier: Base 11 x 11cm (4⅓ x 4⅓in), scored 2.8cm (1¹⁄₁₆in) from each edge; lid 8.5 x 8.5cm (3⅓ x 3⅓in), scored 1.5cm (⅔in) from each edge.

Middle tier: Base 8.7 x 8.7cm (3½ x 3½in), scored 2.6cm (1in) from each edge; lid 7 x 7cm (2¾ x 2¾in) square, scored 1.5cm (⅔in) from each edge.

Top tier: Base 6.5 x 6.5cm (2½ x 2½in), scored 2.1cm (⅘ x ⅘in) from each edge; lid 5 x 5cm (2 x 2in), scored 1.3cm (½ x ½in) from each edge.

2 Trim the edges of each lid with scalloped scissors before gluing. Glue each base together.

3 Cut three pieces of ribbon, 23cm (9in), 15cm (6in) and 11cm (4⅓in) and glue around the base of each box.

4 Punch three large flowers from gold metallic card and three small flowers from brown card. Bend the petals on each and assemble, adding a sticky pearl to the centre of each flower (see detail opposite).

5 Use sticky foam pads to attach the three tier boxes on top of each other and to fix the flowers in position.

Decorate a tube of **wedding bubbles** with a matching punched flower and ribbon bow, each made as before.

Three-tiered Cake
By simply changing the colours of the ribbon and flowers on this favour you can create a more delicate feel. Each box can be used for different gifts, maybe a thank-you note in the top box, after dinner mints in the middle box and a mini silver picture frame in the bottom box.

Crackers for You

Materials:

White glittered silk paper
Crinkled pearl papers
Metallic card
Glitter card
Heart-shaped gemstone
Narrow ribbon
Thick pliable card for the inner
Cracker snap
Sweets or small gift

Tools:

Flower punch
All-purpose glue
Scissors

Instructions:

1 Cut two 20 x 10cm (8 x 4in) rectangles of thick but bendy card. Roll each one up to make a 10cm (4in) tube with a diameter of 3.5cm (1½in). These are your cracker formers and can be reused for all the crackers you make.

2 Cut a 5 x 10cm (2 x 4in) rectangle of bendy card to make the liner. Cut a 13 x 10.5cm (5⅛ x 4⅛in) rectangle of glittered silk paper. Trim your snap to 11cm (4¼in).

3 Place the silk paper face down on your work surface and lay the card liner vertically in the centre. Lay the snap horizontally, in the centre and on top of the liner.

4 Place the two formers in the middle, one lining up with the left hand end of the liner card, the other butting up against the first tube.

5 Apply a line of all-purpose glue to the top edge of the silk paper and liner card, and roll the paper and card firmly around the tubes. Hold while the glue takes.

6 Pull out the left hand former tube by about 2cm (¾in) and tie a piece of ribbon tightly in the gap between the two tubes, pulling in the paper. Remove the left former tube.

7 Place your contents in the cracker by sliding them down the right hand former tube.

8 Pull out the right hand tube so that it leaves a 2cm (¾in) gap between the liner card and former tube. Tie the end as before and remove the tube.

9 Punch five flowers from pearl, glittered and metallic papers and layer. Add a gemstone to the centre and stick to the top of the cracker.

Make a **place card** decorated with a strip of silk paper and a multi-layered punched flower.

Bronzed beauty

An elegant stitched bronze paper is used to make this cracker, with a cream and bronze layered flower. Be sure to choose your paper for cracker making carefully so that it will bend into shape nicely without tearing. Silk-based papers are ideal.

Templates and diagrams

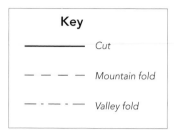

Key

———————— *Cut*

— — — — — *Mountain fold*

— · — · — · *Valley fold*

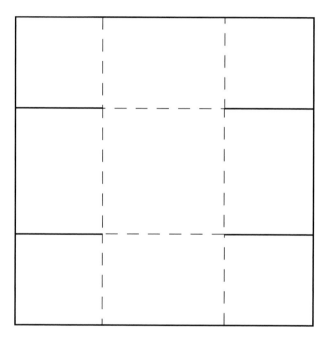

Tying the Knot cutting and folding diagram
(see pages 6–7 for the project).

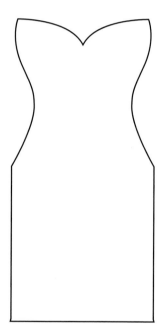

Here Comes The Bride box template
(see pages 22–23 for the project)

Note

This diagram is also used in various different sizes in The Secret Treat! project on pages 42–43. Refer to the instructions on page 43.

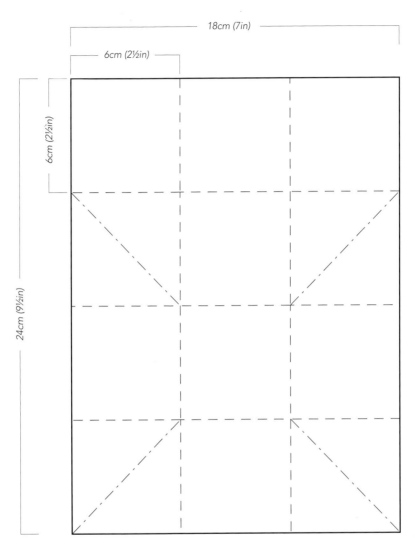

18cm (7in)

6cm (2½in)

6cm (2½in)

24cm (9½in)

Delicrystal cutting and folding diagram
(see pages 18–19 for the project)

Acknowledgements

I would like to thank the team at Search Press for their hard work and dedication. Also, thanks to Mum, Dad and Christian for their never-ending help and support.

Publisher's note

If you would like more books on the ideas and techniques shown, try the following:
Passion for Paper: Paper Punching by Michelle Powell, Search Press, 2008
Design Source Book 26: Wedding Designs by Sonia Griffin, Search Press, 2005
Simple and Stylish Weddings by Jo Rigg, New Holland, 2004